>> contents

why read **this book?**

This is the rule of most perfect Christianity, its most exact definition, its highest point, namely, the seeking of the common good ... for nothing can so make a person an imitator of Christ as caring for his neighbours.

The common good is central to the Christian imagination – in the words of the fourth century preacher, John Chrysostom, 'its highest point' – because God calls people to live in relationship with him and each other.

We live in a time of political turbulence and social division which is challenging our common life. We desperately need a culture of encounter, and the common good offers a way forward for Christians of all traditions. Rooted in relationship with God, we are called to foster a culture of encounter where people who are very different meet each other and estranged groups can be reconciled.

The Old Testament prophet Jeremiah said 'Seek the welfare of the city ... for in its welfare you will find your welfare' (Jeremiah 29.7). It isn't always easy to respond to God's call to live for the common good. It requires us to be people with the courage to 'stay in the room', negotiate and keep dialogue going by recognising the humanity of everyone. By working to make God's vision for the common good a reality we witness to the Good News.

THE COMMON GOOD IN THE BIBLE

This book helps thoughtful Christians explore the common good in the Bible.

We have chosen six short passages which indicate how the Spirit moves us towards relationship and community, how God is concerned for well-being in all areas of society, and how God himself is an 'eternal common good'.

Acts 2 highlights when the first Christians received the Holy Spirit and how the common good is experienced with others—it is a common rather than individual pursuit.

Genesis 11 tells a story of people working together, but for the wrong purpose: they sought their own glory rather than God's.

Amos 5 teaches us that the common good has a spiritual dimension as well as including areas of life like business and legal dealings.

John 17 records Jesus' prayer that 'they may all be one', both because his followers are reconciled to each other and because they know God.

1 Peter 2 makes a strong connection between the common good and witnessing to God. It delves into the Old Testament to show that living for the common good is a model of God's purposes for us all.

Revelation 14 shows an angel proclaiming the eternal Gospel, a vision which reveals the wide range of our work for the common good.

The aim of this book is not to provide neat and tidy answers to all possible questions about the Bible and the common good, but to prompt reflection, discussion and action. These texts provide a good introduction but we are sure you will think of other passages to add colour to the ones suggested here.

It's helpful to note that the 'common good' is at work in various ways in these passages and throughout the Bible. **The common good** can be understood as the

conditions necessary for everyone to thrive, it can also be seen as an **aim** that we aspire to or work for together, and it's also a **practice**, the steps we take to build the common good. This rich conception of the common good clearly shows it is not a utopian ideal as is sometimes thought: it is definitely not something to be imposed by one group on another. At the end of the book you will find a summary of 'Common Good Thinking' which you might like to refer to alongside the scriptural reflections.

CALLING PEOPLE OF GOODWILL

The common good is not simply an idea but something we do together. So the passages are followed by some questions to help you discern what actions you might take, either as an individual or as a group.

God calls all people of goodwill to join in his mission to bless the world. In a time of division and instability we are encouraged to build alliances of goodwill, and we hope and pray that this book blesses you as you respond to God's call to work for the common good.

USING THIS BOOK

Our hope is that the idea of the common good comes alive in the context of personal reflection and conversation with others.

You may like to start by looking at the image and then reading the biblical text slowly and prayerfully.

When you're ready, move onto the reflection.

Choose any or all of the questions. If in a group, allow an hour or so for a good discussion.

When you're ready, say the closing prayer (silently or aloud, as you wish).

It's up to you if you wish to do more than one chapter at a time, or take each one over a number of weeks.

We encourage you to use your favourite version of the Bible. The passages in this book are from the New Revised Standard Version.

NO SPILLS
ANY WAY UP
All who believed were together and had all things in common.
Acts 2.44

all who believed were **together**

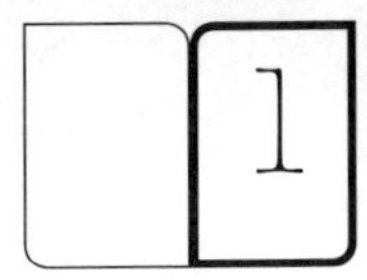

ACTS 2.42-47

[42] They devoted themselves to the apostles' teaching and fellowship, to the breaking of bread and the prayers. [43] Awe came upon everyone, because many wonders and signs were being done by the apostles. [44] All who believed were together and had all things in common; [45] they would sell their possessions and goods and distribute the proceeds to all, as any had need. [46] Day by day, as they spent much time together in the temple, they broke bread at home and ate their food with glad and generous hearts, [47] praising God and having the goodwill of all the people. And day by day the LORD added to their number those who were being saved.

REFLECTION

Luke paints a colourful portrait of the early church. People experience spiritual renewal, witness amazing miracles and stand in awe of God. Luke describes the excitement and dynamism of the new community alongside the radical consequences of experiencing God: 'All who believed were together and had all things in common'.

The early church was quite similar to our churches in that many people didn't have all that much in common. They came from different parts of town and different backgrounds. Just like today, it was tricky to bridge barriers of class and income. Yet, because of God's Holy Spirit, different people sat around the same table. They shared with one another and looked out for each other.

Different people sharing aspirations and projects is the essence of the common good. This sharing can range from negotiating hard to achieve a balance of interests to much cosier relationships. But it always involves people coming together. Just as a language wouldn't exist if people didn't speak with each other, so the common good cannot be achieved alone. Put simply, the common good is only experienced in common with others.

Luke ends his description of the early church with a telling phrase 'And day by day the LORD added to their number those who were being saved'. Not only was it God Himself who saved people and grew the church, but it was God the Holy Spirit who empowered people to live together, sharing food and possessions. This cut against their normal inclinations, just as it does in our day, and Luke wants readers to notice that God surrounds and undergirds the church's common life. By noting how God is involved in helping the community share common aims and live well together, Acts invites us to ask how God is involved in our plans and projects.

|| pause & reflect

Doing things together with others can be quite easy. And it's sometimes really difficult. It involves treating 'the other' as a person loved by God even when that's hard to see. Take a moment to think about what the following statement means to you - 'When you meet another person, you are standing on holy ground.' – Rowan Williams

LORD, show me who you want me to work with.

The new way of life brought about by God's presence had a purpose: to make God known. That the common life of the People of God should witness to God's presence was not a new idea, as we will see. But Luke's picture shows how God's ancient promises take new form in the church. Pentecost shows how God's salvation and reconciliation can transform everyone, whatever their race or background. This transformation is demonstrated by the community's care for its most vulnerable. Then, as now, a mutually supportive, practical common life involving sharing food and alleviating poverty is a bold model for living. Luke notes that it attracted positive attention in wider society, commenting that the church had 'the goodwill of all the people'. We could ask ourselves about the quality of our mutual care, and what it would take for it to be a powerful witness to God's presence among us.

Luke tells of how God's Spirit reinvigorates the life of God's people. As they worship together and seek each other's well-being, they witness to God's presence among them. They seek both God and the good of each other, a common endeavour that gets noticed and so witnesses to God. In our next chapter almost the opposite happens.

QUESTIONS

The following questions will help you reflect further about the common good:

- ? Does any particular verse in the passage strike you as especially relevant to your situation?
- ? In what ways has God been working to sustain the common life of your church and community?
- ? How can you help to build the common good in your church? What practical steps do you need to take to do this?

PRAYERS

Pray for work to build the common good.
The image accompanying this chapter might suggest things to pray for together. Or you could pray in silence.
You may also like to use the following short prayer:

LORD God,
who sends his Spirit upon his people,
and builds his church;
help us to work together,
to build the common good,
and so make you known.
Amen.

Come, let us build ourselves a city, and a tower with its top in the heavens, and let us make a name for ourselves...
Genesis 11.4
INVENTORY
2L80

come, let us build **ourselves** a city

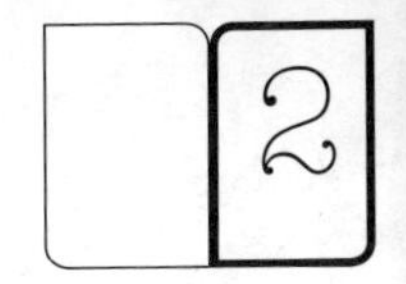

GENESIS 11.1-8

[1] Now the whole earth had one language and the same words. [2] And as they migrated from the east, they came upon a plain in the land of Shinar and settled there. [3] And they said to one another, "Come, let us make bricks, and burn them thoroughly." And they had brick for stone, and bitumen for mortar. [4] Then they said, "Come, let us build ourselves a city, and a tower with its top in the heavens, and let us make a name for ourselves; otherwise we shall be scattered abroad upon the face of the whole earth." [5] The LORD came down to see the city and the tower, which mortals had built. [6] And the LORD said, "Look, they are one people, and they have all one language; and this is only the beginning of what they will do; nothing that they propose to do will now be impossible for them. [7] Come, let us go down, and confuse their language there, so that they will not understand one another's speech." [8] So the LORD scattered them abroad from there over the face of all the earth, and they left off building the city.

REFLECTION

The story of the Tower of Babel mirrors the outpouring of the Holy Spirit at Pentecost. At Pentecost, God gives common purpose and understanding; whereas at Babel, God frustrates people's plans and confuses communication. Yet, like Acts 2, the intriguing tale in Genesis 11 has much to teach us about the common good.

The story starts by highlighting a common endeavour. The thing that stands out, though, is that the people's objective is the wrong one! This wrong decision is the culmination of a series of misguided choices stretching back to the beginning of Genesis. In the beginning God created a world that was good, but Adam and Eve, then Cain, then everyone in the time of Noah, chose badly. Even the new start after the flood didn't change things. Instead of recognising the glory of God's name, Genesis 11 tells how the new residents of the region of Shinar wanted to make a name for themselves by building a tower 'with its top in the heavens'. They had a common project, certainly, but it was in pursuit of their own interests and reputation. We might say that instead of a common good they sought a 'common bad'. Here is a key lesson: working for the common good involves making sure we are pursuing things that are truly good.

If our aims are important, how should they be decided? A feature of doing things with others is that we often don't agree about what to do or how to do it. The processes of negotiation and agreement can be complicated. The Babel project was also the result of negotiation, first to make bricks and then to agree what to do with the bricks. Unfortunately, though, the people didn't consult God about their plans.

Deciding how to live together and making decisions that allow the whole community to flourish takes us into the realm of politics. Politics can be a noble activity if it is practised with a vocation for the common good. Participating in civic society is an important means of forging common bonds, because working together builds community. In a diverse or divided society it is essential.

One of the joys of reading the Bible is its humour, and the Tower of Babel story contains some delightful irony. 'Come', say the people, first to make bricks and then to build a city with a tower whose top reached the heavens. They thought it was so very high, but God says, 'Come, let us go down': he had to descend just to see it! When God descended he saw people pursuing the wrong thing and confounded their communication,

|| pause & reflect

What do you think it looks like to build relationships to overcome mistrust, suspicion or estrangement? What does this teach us about our own need for God? Does my attitude convey that I don't need other people?

Lord, we are all members of one body: give us the courage to tell each other the truth.

so that instead of a language in common the Babel builders shared their need for God.

God's action creates a new architecture for people's relations. His judgement frees them from the dominance of vanity projects, enabling them to decide common aims locally. Perhaps this should make us suspicious of grandiose or utopian visions — of heaven on earth, or earth reaching to heaven — and more sympathetic to embracing many ways of working for good. At the very least, the story of the Tower of Babel prompts us to interrogate our aspirations: are our objectives self-aggrandising or do they serve the common good? Surely this ancient story is one for our times.

Asking pointed questions about our aims helps us stay faithful to God. The Old Testament prophets critiqued and cajoled the people of God for this very reason. In the next chapter we look at how Amos challenged his listeners to seek the common good of justice and fair markets.

QUESTIONS

The following questions will help you reflect further about the common good:

- Does any particular verse in the passage strike you as especially relevant to your situation?
- In what ways has God been working to sustain the common life of your church and community?
- How can you help to build the common good in your church? What practical steps do you need to take to do this?

PRAYERS

Pray for work to build the common good.
The image accompanying this chapter might suggest things to pray for together. Or you could pray in silence. You may also like to use the following short prayer:

God of all,
who looks down upon human endeavours,
and frustrates wrong plans;
reveal to us what is really good,
and plant in us worthwhile aims,
so we can build the common good. Amen.

Hate evil and love good, and establish justice in the gate...
Amos 5.15

establish **justice** in the gate

AMOS 5.14-15a

[14] Seek good and not evil,
 that you may live;
and so the LORD, the God of hosts, will be with you,
 just as you have said.
[15] Hate evil and love good,
 and establish justice in the gate.

REFLECTION

Amos was a prophet. Biblical prophets do not primarily predict the future, but speak God's word to a particular time and place. The prophets point out where things are going wrong in society and direct people to walk in God's ways. Their counsels are based on both the way the world should work, a 'natural morality', and God's special covenant relationship with his people.

Aristotle, the ancient philosopher, said that 'every community is established with a view to some good'; and he argued that the better the good in view, the better the community. This sentiment can be seen in Amos, who urges God's people to choose good instead of evil. Amos recognises that this involves not just individuals but the whole community, a choice summed up in the exhortation to 'establish justice in the gate'.

'The gate' in the towns of Amos' day was not only a thoroughfare and a market, but the place where the heads of families gathered to discuss town politics and, when the need arose, to deal with misdemeanours — it served as a court house. In this chapter, Amos says that two things distort right legal decisions. The first is hatred towards those who speak unpalatable truths 'in the gate'. An example of such animosity would be discrediting a person who protects the innocent by telling the truth (Amos 5.10). The second way Amos says that legal processes are distorted is by the rich bribing witnesses or the elders to obtain favourable verdicts (Amos 5.12). Both actions prejudice the innocent and powerless. In the face of such injustices, Amos exhorts elders to take just decisions that serve the cause of justice. We see that the well-being of society, the common good, requires an unimpeachable justice system that is sustained by individuals choosing to act rightly.

If working for justice involves the whole community, so does maintaining a 'moral market', another of Amos' great concerns. Despite military stability and economic prosperity, the country was riven by inequality as a result of the rich taking advantage of the poor. Although markets are usually conceived as places for the exchange of private goods and services, a system of fair exchange is itself a good. In fact, fair markets are a common good that require everyone to act in an ethical and virtuous way if they are to function well.

Amos highlights how this hasn't happened. He shines a spotlight on dishonest dealing and deception, describing how such practices 'trample on the needy and bring to ruin the poor of the land' (Amos 8.4). Amos' language is poetic and shocking, describing how God will destroy the houses and farms of oppressors. But at the very end of the book, there is a hopeful vision of a society — a wealthy society, not one that is less prosperous — characterised by a moral market. Workers are allowed to rest on the Sabbath, for example, and people realise it is in their interests to treat each other as they would be done by.

pause & reflect

Spend some time quietly reflecting on the following passage:

'Seek the welfare of the city ... because in its welfare you will find your welfare.'
Jeremiah 29.7

Lord, show me how to help create a just society.

In Amos 5.14-15 God features prominently. God is the one who will be present, who will be gracious and is concerned for justice. In other words, God is interested in the good that the community has in view and how it is pursued — once again, we see that there is a spiritual dimension to the common good. The prophets tell truths about God and justice, and they speak about how to create a just society where all thrive. Jesus said many similar things, one reason why the words of the prophets are still relevant for Christians, and others, today. In the next chapter we will look more closely at Jesus' prayer the night before he died to understand the spiritual aspect of the common good more deeply.

QUESTIONS

The following questions will help you reflect further about the common good:

- **?** Amos presents a stark choice between good and evil. Do you think that our choices are always this clear? What are the implications of your answer for seeking the common good?
- **?** Working for just laws, justly applied, is a crucial aspect of building the common good. Is there anything you could do to further this cause (e.g. becoming a magistrate or writing in support of prisoners who have been unjustly incarcerated)?
- **?** Building moral markets can entail doing business with integrity, participating as ethical savers and investors, helping those who have fallen victim to debt through dishonest dealing or making wrong choices, or campaigning for adequate conditions of employment. What practical things could you do in your context?

PRAYERS

Pray for work to build the common good.
The image accompanying this chapter might suggest things to pray for together. Or you could pray in silence. You may also like to use the following short prayer:

God of justice,
who promises to have mercy;
enable us: to seek good not evil,
establish justice where we are,
sustain moral markets,
and know your presence among us.
Amen.

I ask not only on behalf of these, but also on behalf of those who will believe in me through their word, that they may all be one...
John 17.20

that they may all be **one**

4

JOHN 17.20-24

[20] I ask not only on behalf of these, but also on behalf of those who will believe in me through their word, [21] that they may all be one. As you, Father, are in me and I am in you, may they also be in us, so that the world may believe that you have sent me. [22] The glory that you have given me I have given them, so that they may be one, as we are one, [23] I in them and you in me, that they may become completely one, so that the world may know that you have sent me and have loved them even as you have loved me. [24] Father, I desire that those also, whom you have given me, may be with me where I am, to see my glory, which you have given me because you loved me before the foundation of the world.

REFLECTION

Our prayers reveal what we care about. Jesus' prayer for oneness reflects his deepest concerns the night before he died. It illuminates the common good in surprising ways.

The fact that Jesus prays to his Father is significant, for it points to the importance of faith. This is not just any old faith, however, for Jesus' prayer is directed towards a particular person: his faith is in God the Father. The Gospel of John insists that God loves all people and wants everyone to know him (see especially John 3.16). The words in this passage explain that this means being one with Jesus and the Father. So these verses, just like other Bible passages we have looked at, point to God as the eternal common good.

Because Jesus prays that everyone will have faith in God and be one with him, working for the common good involves dialogue about the spiritual dimension of life. These conversations must be respectful of others' convictions, including religious convictions, of course. But they will not avoid what it means to be made in the image of God and how life in all its fullness (See John 10.10) includes knowing God. You may like to think about how your conversations could be like this.

The main theme of Jesus' prayer is 'one-ness'. The very fact that he asks for unity between the disciples indicates that there was disunity. Jesus repeats himself for emphasis: the concern of his prayer is that through his own relationship with the Father people can be reconciled to God and to each other.

Jesus prays that reconciliation between the disciples is achieved so effectively that they share a common identity. Christians of different traditions are often quick to notice their differences. But Jesus prays that those who share a faith be as one because they have God's glory in common. This resonates with the concern expressed in other parts of the Bible that people use their gifts for the good of all (see 1 Corinthians 12.7). Are there new ways in which we could work with others because of our common identity?

Many churches are involved in bridging divides, often because they contain people from all walks of life, as we saw when looking at the early church in Acts. The practical work of reconciliation is central to building the common good. Yet it can be tough. Attempting to hold together parties that pull in different directions can require tact, insight and courage. It requires people of goodwill who are willing to work together, across social, religious and political differences. Jesus himself suggests that one-ness is something that will take time: it means being realistic, recognising the difficulties of building bonds of peace, and persevering for the good of all.

The reconciled one-ness Jesus prays for is not an end in itself but serves a wider mission. Jesus asks that the unity of a community whose members are reconciled to one another should witness to Jesus' own reconciling work. His vision is that as a result

|| pause & reflect

Who are the invisible people in our community?

Am I listening closely enough to people doing humble, manual tasks, or who are poor, ill or old?

Have I looked down on people who disagree with me?

Lord, show me how I can help to heal divisions in my community.

of the believers' one-ness, the world will come to know God's love. This is an important theme and in the next chapter we see how some of the first Christians were encouraged to see themselves as mission-minded by their very nature.

QUESTIONS

The following questions will help you reflect further about the common good:

- ? What does it mean for you that God is the eternal common good? How might this affect how you speak with people about faith?
- ? Working with others for the common good is a response to Jesus' prayer. How can our common identity in Christ help in working with others?
- ? What joys and challenges have you experienced when building bridges or being reconciled with others? Do you have any hints or tips for others in this important work?

PRAYERS

Pray for work to build the common good.
The image accompanying this chapter might suggest things to pray for together. Or you could pray in silence. You may also like to use the following short prayer:

God of glory,
Father, Son and Holy Spirit;
give us faith
to take risks for the common good,
and to be reconciled with each other,
so that we can be one with you.

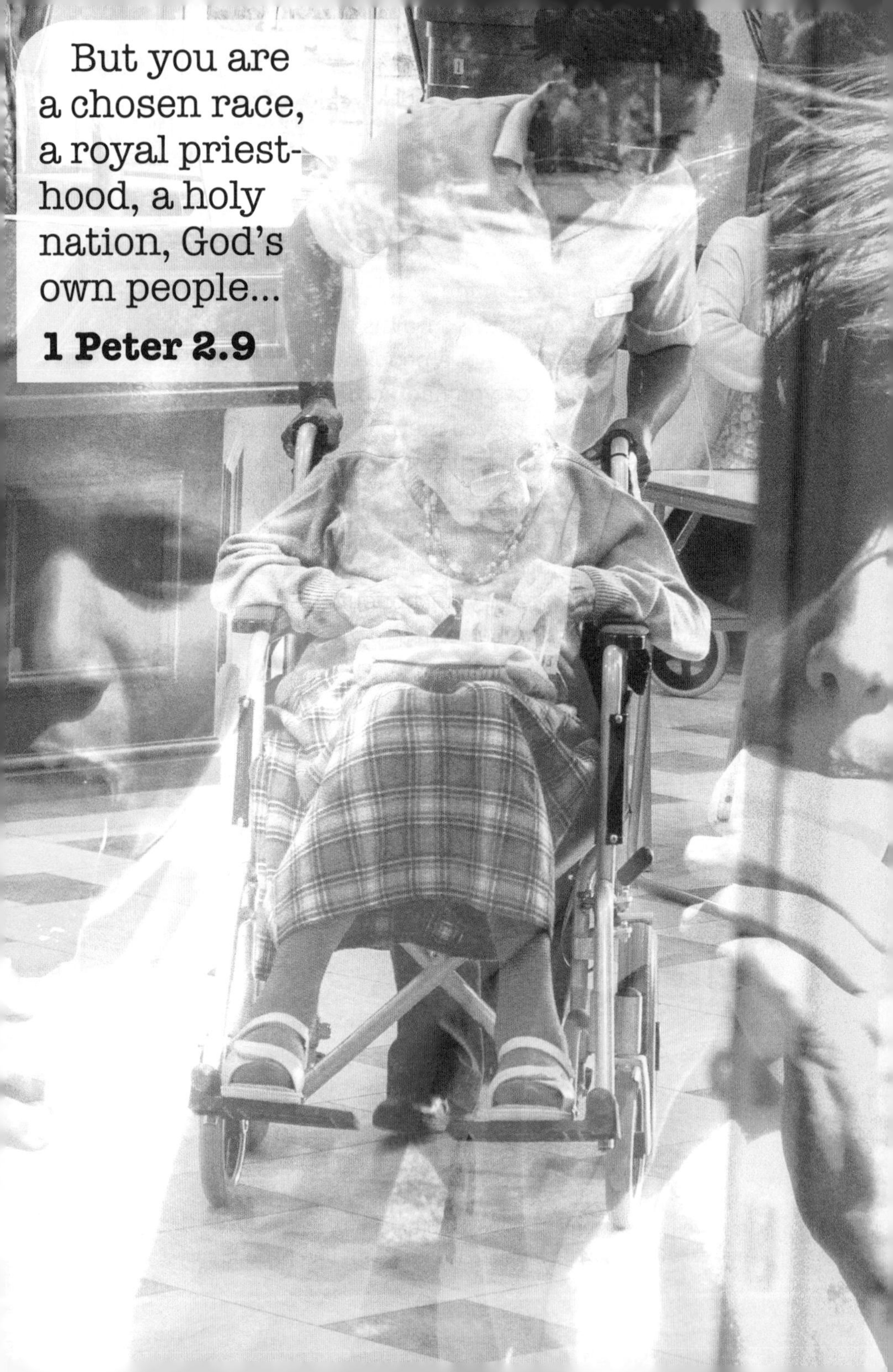
But you are
a chosen race,
a royal priest-
hood, a holy
nation, God's
own people...
1 Peter 2.9

you are **God's people**

1 PETER 2.9-12

[9] But you are a chosen race, a royal priesthood, a holy nation, God's own people, in order that you may proclaim the mighty acts of him who called you out of darkness into his marvellous light. [10] Once you were not a people, but now you are God's people; once you had not received mercy, but now you have received mercy. [11] Beloved, I urge you as aliens and exiles to abstain from the desires of the flesh that wage war against the soul. [12] Conduct yourselves honourably among the Gentiles, so that, though they malign you as evildoers, they may see your honourable deeds and glorify God when he comes to judge.

REFLECTION

This verse is all about the mission of God and his people. It speaks of how our life together witnesses to God's mighty acts of rescue. The list of things that the Church is — chosen race, royal priesthood, holy nation and God's own people — explains how we are witnesses.

Peter's statement does not come out of thin air, but alludes to a much older part of scripture. In Exodus 19 we read that Moses goes up a mountain to talk with God, who instructs him to remind the people they have already been rescued from slavery in Egypt. In the Bible, people are frequently urged to remember what God has done. And Jesus gave bread and wine to his disciples with the words 'Do this in remembrance of me'. There's an important lesson here: recalling God's goodness can inspire us to work for the common good.

The passage in Exodus uses the very words Peter employs in his letter. In the Old Testament, the people of God were called 'treasured possession', 'royal priesthood' and 'holy nation'. Now, Peter calls Christian communities the very same things. 'God's own people' is synonymous with being a 'treasured possession', but what do the other terms mean?

'A royal priesthood' belongs to the king, in this case, God Himself. But why is a people called a priesthood? A priest is an intermediary, someone who stands between God and people. By calling the whole People of God a priesthood, Moses and then Peter indicate that this community mediates between God and the world. So rather than being chosen simply to receive blessings and keep them to themselves, the people are called to make God's blessings known. This is crystal clear in the prophecy of Isaiah, which says that the chosen race are to declare God's praises (see Isaiah 43.20-21).

They do this by being a holy nation. A holy nation is a distinctive people. Both the Old and New Testaments trace the origins of this distinctiveness to God and his rescue. The Bible affirms that a community that has been rescued by God should take care of others. The word most often used to describe this mutual solidarity is 'justice'. This is the relational vision behind biblical teaching. And because a just society is key to human flourishing, the Bible frequently condemns injustice. So, a good common life requires each of us to take responsibility to work for social justice by building relationships and valuing every human person.

|| pause & reflect

Take a moment to recall some of the ways in which God's goodness has prompted you to work for the common good where you live.

Thank God for his inspiration.

Lord, give me the courage to listen and look for common ground in unexpected places.

Often counter-cultural, our mission involves protecting the vulnerable, including the excluded, and serving the wider community. This is because being a holy nation not only witnesses to God's past salvation, but also serves as a model of how things could be.

1 Peter 2.9 leads us in this direction. Just as 'There's light at the end of the tunnel', God's marvellous light is at the end of the verse. The people of God are described as a chosen race, holy nation, royal priesthood and God's own people because they have experienced God's light. And their mission is to make this light shine everywhere through the way they live their lives. In fact, verse 12 ties together how we live and the church's public witness very strongly: 'Conduct

yourselves honourably among the Gentiles, so that, though they malign you as evildoers, they may see your honourable deeds and glorify God when he comes to judge'.

Since God's glory cannot be seen, it is often described as radiant light; it is a metaphor for God himself. The final book of the Bible paints a picture of a new heaven and a new earth with God at the centre. In the final chapter we will look at how this hopeful vision helps us understand yet more aspects of the common good.

QUESTIONS

The following questions will help you reflect further about the common good:

? Working for social justice is an important part of working for the common good. How have you seen this take shape in your town or locality? As part of its mission, is your church involved in nurturing new social enterprises or helping those who need support?

? How do you respond to the idea that churches mediate the knowledge of God by the way Christians live their lives? Are there any lessons to be learnt from past successes or failures?

? In what ways does your Christian hope shape your life?

PRAYERS

Pray for work to build the common good.
The image accompanying this chapter might suggest things to pray for together. Or you could pray in silence. You may also like to use the following short prayer:

God of mission,
help us to live well together:
loving our neighbours,
and working for justice;
so that our common life witnesses to your goodness,
and makes you known among all nations.

Then I saw another angel flying in mid-heaven, with an eternal gospel to proclaim to those who live on the earth...

Revelation 14.6

an **eternal** gospel

REVELATION 14.6-7

[6] Then I saw another angel flying in mid-heaven, with an eternal gospel to proclaim to those who live on the earth—to every nation and tribe and language and people. [7] He said in a loud voice, "Fear God and give him glory, for the hour of his judgment has come; and worship him who made heaven and earth, the sea and the springs of water.

REFLECTION

We live in a world saturated by images, making Revelation, which offers dramatic almost cinematic visions, a book for our days.

In Revelation 14.6-7 the author sees an angel. Listen to the eternal good news that the angel proclaims to the four corners of the earth: 'Fear God and give Him glory'. This means placing God first and giving him due weight in our lives, in other words, worshipping him. Right at the end of the Bible in the angel's proclamation to 'every nation and tribe and language and people' we hear the echo that has resonated through its pages: God is the eternal common good.

It's perhaps rather more surprising, however, to read that the eternal Gospel involves God's judgement. God's judgement, though, is not like a celestial referee dispensing heavenly red cards. It is about putting things right; in short, of establishing God's justice. This is why the persecuted churches of Revelation are offered God's judgement as a source of hope in an unjust world.

We have already seen that the Bible is very concerned that people act justly, and that working for justice is a key aspect of building the common good. The eternal Gospel's reference to creation points back to Genesis and God's declaration that the world he made was 'very good'. Among other things, this means that there are firm foundations for what is right and wrong. They are not simply culturally determined or what powerful people decide, but have their roots in the way God has made things. Thus the common good is objectively good — it doesn't just depend on the loudest voices saying so. In fact, we should be suspicious of claims by particular interest groups that something is good — quite often it's especially good for them. Similarly, we can question the motivations of those who claim to be working for the common good yet refuse to work with others.

We have seen that God's judgement is good news and not a big stick because it is God putting things right. This re-creation is highlighted by the images of the sea and springs of water. These are perhaps unexpected in an eternal gospel, for we tend to think 'eternal' things are not only timeless but formless, too. Yet God's vindication of his initial judgement to create the world in a particular way invites us to care for his creation. In fact, caring for God's creation is part of building the common good because creation is common to everyone and integral to human flourishing. Although some, through luck or providence, will be able to benefit to a greater extent than others, the Bible is clear that exploitation of the land by a few for their own profit is not to be tolerated.

The angel's message is proclaimed throughout the world because everyone is valued by God and so can respond to the eternal gospel. So it follows that all people regardless of background have a responsibility to contribute to the common good — from the grassroots to the boardroom. Thus there are no grounds for excluding others because they are different from us. This can be challenging, of course. But as we work together, we offer a counter-cultural picture to the world: an example of people living in the light of an eternal gospel.

|| pause & reflect

God saw everything that he had made, and, indeed, it was very good. Genesis 1.31

Lord, when the Bible ceases to challenge me, please help me to listen more closely.

QUESTIONS

The following questions will help you reflect further about the common good:

- How do you hope for God to establish his justice in the world?
- Are we prepared to work with others to build the common good? Do you think this is a good test of our commitment to working for God's justice?
- Caring for the environment and building sustainable communities is important for both ourselves and future generations. This may involve anything from driving less to making choices that support family life. What practical steps can you take in your context to care for the world around you?

PRAYERS

Pray for work to build the common good.
The image accompanying this chapter might suggest things to pray for together. Or you could pray in silence.
You may also like to use the following short prayer:

Eternal God,
who made all things,
and puts all things right;
help us to put you first,
and work with everyone of goodwill,
as we respond to your call: to pursue the common good.
Amen.

common good thinking

Our reflections on the common good in the Bible have revealed a number of talking points. Among the most significant is that God is the eternal common good. For this reason, working for the common good is a foretaste of our future hope.

Building the common good involves collaborating with other people of goodwill. This may require reconciliation of different interests. It certainly will involve taking practical steps with others to create communities where all can flourish.

The Bible identifies many areas of life in which seeking the common good is essential for a healthy society, including good legal processes, social justice, economic opportunity and creation care – the common good has wide relevance.

It is possible to identify these biblical themes in the thought of many different cultures and traditions, from Aristotle to Ubuntu and Shalom, in humanist traditions and in Jewish teaching. These common themes are particularly well expressed in Catholic Social Thought, a body of thinking exploring how Gospel values can take shape in society. It is attracting increasing interest across different Christian denominations, other faith traditions and non-religious groups too. The five headline principles of common good thinking can be found on the next page.

common good thinking

Rooted in Gospel values, these principles can help us as we build our common life together

THE COMMON GOOD

The common good is itself a principle to be applied along with the other principles here.

The common good is the set of conditions in which every individual in the community can flourish. But the creation of those conditions is something we do, and need to do together, so we can also talk about the practice of the common good. This involves everyone participating fully and taking responsibility according to their vocation and ability. The common good is not a utopian ideal to be imposed by one 'enlightened' group upon another: it involves building relationships between those with different views and experiences, and balancing their different interests. Simply put, 'it is in all our interests that all thrive.'

THE PERSON

Common good thinking highlights these important aspects of the human person:

Human Dignity: Every person is worthy of respect simply by virtue of being a human being.

Human Equality: All human beings are of equal worth in the eyes of God.

Dignity of Work: Work is more than a way to make a living – it is good for our humanity, because through work we participate in God's creative plan.

Respect for Life: People matter more than things: each human life has value, from the youngest to the oldest, from the weakest to the strongest.